TO LOVE AND SERVE

Lectionary-Based Meditations
Year A

Gerald Darring

Sheed & Ward

BX
2170
.C55
D369
1994

Also available from Sheed & Ward:
- *To Love and Serve: Lectionary-Based Meditations for Year B,*
- *To Love and Serve: Lectionary-Based Meditations for Year C,*
    —*both by Gerald Darring*

Copyright© 1994 by Gerald Darring

All rights reserved. No part of this book may be reproduced or transmitted in any form or by any means, electronic or mechanical, including photocopying, recording or by an information storage and retrieval system without permission in writing from the Publisher.

Sheed & Ward™ is a service of The National Catholic Reporter Publishing Company.

ISBN: 1-55612-701-4

Published by: Sheed & Ward
            115 E. Armour Blvd.
            P.O. Box 419492
            Kansas City, MO 64141

To order, call: (800) 333-7373

INTRODUCTION

The liturgy should be a major source of spiritual growth for Catholics. The spirit of our worship should permeate our entire lives, and the readings, prayers, songs, and ritual actions of our liturgy should influence the way we think and act. These meditations are presented in this spirit.

There is a meditation for each Sunday of the liturgical year as well as for those feasts which are celebrated in place of the normal Sunday liturgy. Each meditation is placed within the context of the Scriptures on the one hand and the contemporary teaching of the Church on the other. Passages taken from the Sunday liturgy are placed in italics: they can be from one of the Scriptural readings or from a prayer, antiphon, psalm, or preface.

The meditations have an overall focus outward toward the world served by the Church. The general aim is to aid the individual Catholic in becoming more Scripturally and liturgically grounded as he or she struggles to come to grips with the personal and social challenges of life in our time and to accept the challenge given at the end of every Mass to *go in peace to love and serve the Lord.*

I dedicate this book to my son, Matthew Gerald, whom I greatly admire for his originality, his love of nature, and his gentle ways.

CONTENTS

Advent	1
Christmas	7
Ordinary Time after Epiphany	13
Lent	23
Easter	31
Ordinary Time after Pentecost	41
Feasts	69

ADVENT

1st Sunday in Advent

Readings: Isaiah 2:1-5
Romans 13:11-14
Matthew 24:37-44

The Son of Man is coming at the time you least expect. That is a frightening prospect. What if Jesus comes when there are still nearly two and a half billion people living in countries where the annual per capita income is $400 or less? when there are still about 40,000 people dying every day from hunger? when a billion people, one fifth of the human race, still do not have decent housing? when there are still 20 million Latin American children sleeping in the street? when there are still hundreds of millions of people without basic medical care? when one out of every four human beings still has no access to safe drinking water? when we are still burning down rain forests, depleting the ozone layer that protects us from the sun, depositing black crude oil along the delicate shoreline of the world, sending noxious gasses into the atmosphere so they return to earth as acid rain and pollute lakes and streams, playing games with radioactive materials that will be around to torture us for centuries?

It is now the hour for us to wake from sleep. The challenge to *beat our swords into plowshares* has been around for centuries, as have other biblical challenges to *cast off deeds of darkness.* The season of Advent is a time for us to awaken ourselves so that we can better prepare for the coming of Christ.

"Hope in the coming kingdom is already beginning to take root in the hearts of men. The radical transformation of the world in the paschal mystery of the Lord gives full meaning to the efforts of men, and in particular of the young, to lessen injustice, violence and hatred and to advance all together in justice, freedom, brotherhood and love." Synod of Bishops, *Justice in the World* (1971) 76.

2nd Sunday in Advent

Readings: Isaiah 11:1-10
Romans 15:4-9
Matthew 3:1-12

Today's gospel shows John the Baptist clashing with the Jewish religious authorities. We see the Pharisees and Sadducees stepping forward to be baptized by John. These people "did not believe him" (Matthew 21:32), but they came forward anyway, boasting of the claim that *Abraham is our father*. John recognized them for what they were, people of privilege who applaud social justice only insofar as it applies to them. *Give some evidence that you mean to reform*, he told them. He did not object to their coming forward; he objected to their lack of concern for real change in society.

In his brief discourse to the Pharisees and Sadducees, John described the action that was taking place: *Even now the ax is laid to the root of the tree. Every tree that is not fruitful will be cut down and thrown into the fire.* John's message was about justice, about social change. He challenged the people of Israel to get down to the root causes of problems, to uproot unfruitful trees.

The changes that are called for in Advent are fundamental and far-reaching; they are structural. In this new church year, we are challenged to work for a better society, different from the one we now have.

"The uniqueness of the Christian message does not so much consist in the affirmation of the necessity for structural change, as it does in the insistence on the conversion of people which will in turn bring about this change. We will not have a new continent without new and reformed structures, but, above all, there will be no new continent without new people, who know how to be truly free and responsible according to the light of the Gospel." Bishops of Latin America, Medellin Documents, *Justice* (1968) 3.

3rd Sunday in Advent

Readings: Isaiah 35:1-6, 10
James 5:7-10
Matthew 11:2-11

From his cell in prison John the Baptist had heard stories about Jesus, and he sent some of his followers to find out if Jesus is the messiah. *Are you 'He who is to come' or do we look for another?* they asked Jesus. Jesus had to reply in such a way that John would have no doubt about the genuineness of his messianic activity, and the message he sent back to John was about the blind receiving their sight, the lame walking, the lepers being cleansed, the deaf hearing, the dead being raised, and the poor having good news brought to them. He did not say a word about people praying more or going to the synagogue or making God the center of their lives: The age of the messiah, as expressed in this report, does not concern "religion" in the traditional sense of the word. One knows that the messiah has come because a real change has taken place in society, a change that involves the liberation of those who have always been cut off from the 'main branch' of society. Jesus is the messiah because those who are blind, crippled, diseased, and poor have been liberated from the things which make them the victims of injustice. We can turn the statement around to say that if the dregs of society do not experience liberation, then Jesus is not the messiah. But Jesus is the messiah, and so the dead have come to life: those who have been unable to 'live' in a society that has written them off, are now alive with hope.

"The gospel has truly been a leaven of liberty and progress in human history, even in its temporal sphere, and always proves itself a leaven of brotherhood, of unity, and of peace. Therefore, not without cause is Christ hailed by the faithful as 'the expected of the nations, and their Savior' (Antiphon O for Dec. 23)." Vatican II, *Decree on the Missionary Activity of the Church* (1965) 8.

4th Sunday in Advent

Readings: Isaiah 7:10-14
Romans 1:1-7
Matthew 1:18-24

Today's liturgy is about God with us, Emmanuel. We have arrived at the moment of the celebration of God's presence within the human family. The Emmanuel of Advent-Christmas, the God who is with us, witnesses our social life from within the community, so that God is not far away but is actually among us as we become part of each others lives (and sometimes step on them), as we work together (and sometimes against each other), as we try to support each other (and yet abandon millions of people to the miseries of destitution). There is no childish game of hide and seek with this God, who is present to witness our good deeds and our misdeeds.

Let the Lord enter. We rejoice at the prospect of having God among us, and yet we should also reflect on the awesome responsibility of living in the presence of God. We *who have been called to belong to Jesus Christ* should imitate Mary, who, when faced with the reality of Emmanuel, *placed her life at the service of God's plan.*

"Seeking after the glory of Christ, the Church becomes more like her exalted model, and continually progresses in faith, hope, and charity, searching out and doing the will of God in all things. Hence the Church in her apostolic work also rightly looks to her who brought forth Christ, conceived by the Holy Spirit and born of the Virgin, so that through the Church Christ may be born and grow in the hearts of the faithful also." Vatican II, *Constitution on the Church* (1964) 65.

CHRISTMAS

Christmas

Readings: Isaiah 62:1-5 Acts 13:16-17, 22-25 Matthew 1:1-25
Isaiah 9:1-6 Titus 2:11-14 Luke 2:1-14
Isaiah 62:11-12 Titus 3:4-7 Luke 2:15-20
Isaiah 52:7-10 Hebrews 1:1-6 John 1:1-18

The first people to experience the coming of the savior were shepherds, those lowly, uneducated ones who lived among the animals. They were not the only ones, of course, but they were the first to welcome the savior.

It was no accident that such lowly people would be called in first to pay homage to the savior. It is to the lowly, after all, that Christ came first as Lord and Redeemer. The circumstances of his birth testify to that: his mother *wrapped him in swaddling clothes and laid him in a manger, because there was no room for them in the place where travelers lodged.*

Christmas is the great annual renewal of our being a Church *filled with wonder at the nearness of her God.* The nearer we are to our God, the nearer we should become to those lowly ones who are God's special ones. We are challenged at Christmas to do what Jesus and the angels did: bring the good news of redemption to the outcast and the lowly. The *tidings of great joy (are) to be shared by the whole people,* and no one is to be left out, not even the most hopeless or despicable person.

"Our holy Mother (the Church does) not neglect the care of the poor or omit to provide for their necessities; but, rather, drawing them to her with a mother's embrace, and knowing that they bear the person of Christ Himself, who regards the smallest gift to the poor as a benefit conferred on Himself, holds them in great honor. She does all she can to help them; she provides homes and hospitals where they may be received, nourished, and cared for all the world over, and watches over these." Pope Leo XIII, *Quod Apostolici Muneris* (1878) 9.

Holy Family

Readings: Sirach 3:2-6, 12-14
Colossians 3:12-21
Matthew 2:13-15, 19-23

We can be critical of the old family structure reflected in the command for wives to be submissive to their husbands, but we must admit that the old structure worked in many ways. Families were stable social units, contributing much to the right ordering of society.

We no longer feel comfortable with wives being submissive to husbands, and just the reading of this passage in today's liturgy offends some people. Perhaps we ought to accept this reading as a challenge to find a new family structure that works. The alternative to the old family structure should not be an absence of structure resulting in the breakdown of the family; rather, it should be a new family structure built around mutual love and equal partnership.

The celebration of the Holy Family should serve as a reminder to us that the family is holy; that there is a reflection of our Trinitarian God in the father, mother and child of the family; and that there will be no order in society if there is not stability in family life.

"As a nation, we need to make children and families our first priority, to invest in their future, to combat the forces—cultural, economic and moral—which hurt children and destroy families; to manage our economy, shape our government, and direct our institutions to support and not undermine our families." U.S. Bishops, *Putting Children and Families First: A Challenge for Our Church, Nation and World* (1991) IV.

Mary, Mother of God (Jan 1)

Readings: Numbers 6:22-27
Galatians 4:4-7
Luke 2:16-21

Mary treasured all these things and reflected on them in her heart.

"All these things" happened to be a remarkable collection of circumstances: the conception of a child in her virginity; the census call to report to Bethlehem, King David's hometown; the lack of room in town just at the time of the birth of her child; the visit by shepherds with startling news of a vision of angels; and the naming of the child "Yahweh saves." Mary *treasured* these things and *reflected on them in her heart.*

Parents teach children what they need to know. Mary, the Mother of God and our mother, teaches us to treasure the wonderful presence of God in the midst of poverty, homelessness, and discrimination. She teaches us to reflect in our hearts, not on the darkness but on the light that shines on us this day.

May we always profit by the prayers of the Virgin Mother Mary. May we also profit by the example of her life as she treasured the events of our salvation unfolding before her and reflected on them in her heart.

"Jesus takes the side of those most in need, physically and spiritually. The example of Jesus ... calls for an emptying of self, both individually and corporately, that allows the Church to experience the power of God in the midst of poverty and powerlessness." U.S. Bishops, *Economic Justice for All* (1986) 52.

Epiphany

Readings: Isaiah 60:1-6
Ephesians 3:2-3, 5-6
Matthew 2:1-12

The "epiphany" of Jesus, his revelation to the world, was accompanied by the offering of three gifts, each of which symbolized a different aspect of the divine/human savior. Frankincense is offered to Jesus, the Son of God, the eternal Word of the Father who is worshipped with the Father and the Spirit. Gold is offered to Jesus the King of the human race, the summit of creation. Myrrh is offered to the divine/human savior of the world who suffered and died for the salvation of all.

Jesus is revealed in our own day. He is revealed as the Word of God speaking to us in the marvelous workings of nature, in the achievements of the human spirit, and in the dialogue between Church and world. He is revealed to us as King in every victory over ignorance, alienation and powerlessness. He is revealed to us as Suffering Messiah in the heart and face of every poor person, every stranger, every wanderer living in a back alley or under a bridge, every person victimized by others.

His glory has shone among us. We have only to recognize him and to do what the magi did in his presence: *They prostrated themselves and did him homage.*

"Jesus perfected revelation by fulfilling and manifesting himself: through his words and deeds, his signs and wonders, but especially through his death and glorious resurrection from the dead and final sending of the Spirit of truth." Vatican II, *Constitution on Divine Revelation* (1965) 4.

ORDINARY TIME AFTER EPIPHANY

The Baptism of the Lord

Readings: Isaiah 42:1-4, 6-7
Acts 10:34-38
Matthew 3:13-17

The baptism of Jesus by John the Baptist was an embarrassment to the early church. John, after all, was the precursor to Jesus: why should Jesus be baptized by him? And Jesus was sinless: how could he be "washed" of any sinfulness? Only Mark presents the event in a simple and straightforward way. Matthew and Luke soften its impact in their versions, and John leaves it out completely.

The scholarly consensus is that the baptism actually took place and was preserved by the early church in spite of its misgivings. One way to understand the baptism of the Lord would be to see it as a link between the exodus passage through water to the promised land and the sacramental passage through the water of baptism to salvation in Jesus Christ. Jesus acted out the same passage through water that has been undertaken by others since the beginning of salvation history.

The world must be washed of all that makes it unclean: alienation from God and from each other; attacks against life and against the author of life; the oppression of God's children and the destruction of God's creation. The world must pass through the same waters of salvation that Jews and Christians have passed through.

"The Church, now sojourning on earth as an exile, is necessary for salvation. For Christ, made present to us in his Body, which is the Church, is the one Mediator and the unique Way of salvation. In explicit terms he himself affirmed the necessity of faith and baptism and thereby affirmed also the necessity of the Church, for through baptism as through a door men enter the Church." Vatican II, *Constitution on the Church* (1964) 14.

2nd Sunday in Ordinary Time

Readings: Isaiah 49:3, 5-6
1 Corinthians 1:1-3
John 1:29-34

In today's Gospel, John sees Jesus and exclaims: *Look there! The Lamb of God who takes away the sin of the world!* He doesn't say "the sins of the world;" he uses the singular: "the sin of the world" (*peccatum* in Latin, *ten hamarten* in Greek).

We all sin, and we sin in different ways and at different times. We can speak of "sins" (in the plural), but all our sins are of a piece: they are different manifestations of our sinfulness. The liturgy alternates between these two perspectives, acknowledging that "you take away the sin of the world" (Glory to God) and also that "you take away the sins of the world" (Lamb of God).

The recently developed concept of social sin is an attempt to articulate the sinfulness of humankind. It isn't just that we do wrong things: the fact is that we are basically "off center." It is our "original" sin that matters most, our fundamental option for ourselves over and above God. The rest is expression, like coloring the picture or connecting the dots.

The wonder of Jesus is that he takes away not only the sins but also the sin. He fills us with the Spirit of sinlessness, the Spirit that will *make us one in peace and love.*

"The disturbances which so frequently occur in the social order result in part from the natural tensions of economic, political, and social forms. But at a deeper level they flow from man's pride and selfishness, which contaminate even the social sphere." Vatican II, *Constitution on the Church in the Modern World* (1965) 25.

3rd Sunday in Ordinary Time

Readings: Isaiah 8:23—9:3
1 Corinthians 1:10-13, 17
Matthew 4:12-23

In today's Gospel Matthew applies to Jesus the prophetic oracle of Isaiah: *The people who walked in darkness have seen a great light; upon those who dwelt in the land of gloom a light has shone.* In like manner, the psalmist's assertion that *the Lord is my light* is echoed in Jesus' words: *I am the light of the world; the man who follows me will have the light of life.*

Christianity is about light. Just as Jesus is light to the world, so his church is to be light in a world of darkness. Light enables the beauty of things to be seen, and we are called to make the beauty of the world shine. But we are not to call attention to ourselves: if you are aware of the light in a room, it is too bright. Our vocation is for others, not ourselves.

Surrounded by discrimination, oppression and war, Christians are challenged to *be united in mind and judgment,* and they are directed by God's love to *bring mankind to unity and peace.* The light we bring to the world should lead in time to an end of all the world's darkness: the alienation and oppression of peoples, the attacks on human life and dignity, and disrespect for God's creation.

A people living in darkness has seen a great light.

"The Church... serves as a leaven and as a kind of soul for human society as it is to be renewed in Christ and transformed into God's family.... the Church not only communicates divine life to men, but in some way casts the reflected light of that life over the entire earth." Vatican II, *Constitution on the Church in the Modern World* (1965) 40.

4th Sunday in Ordinary Time

Readings: Zephaniah 2:3; 3:12-13
1 Corinthians 1:26-31
Matthew 5:1-12

Today's liturgy is about love: *help us to love you with all our hearts and to love all men as you love them.* It is also about justice: we are to *seek justice*, following the Lord, who *secures justice for the oppressed*, and following Christ, whom God has made *our wisdom and also our justice.*

But God's love and justice are different from ours. The Gospel teaches us that in the just world of God, the sorrowing are consoled, the lowly inherit the land, the hungry have their fill, and the persecuted rejoice at being insulted and slandered. The children of God are different from the children of the world: *God chose those whom the world considers absurd to shame the wise; he singled out the weak of this world to shame the strong. He chose the world's lowborn and despised, those who count for nothing, to reduce to nothing those who were something.*

The love of God is more powerful than all the sin we can muster, and the justice of God overcomes all the world's injustice, its poverty and hunger, its oppression and war, its alienation and domination of others. *The Lord sets captives free.* May we be saved by the Lord's love.

"Christian love of neighbor and justice cannot be separated. For love implies an absolute demand for justice, namely a recognition of the dignity and rights of one's neighbor. Justice attains its inner fullness only in love. Because every man is truly a visible image of the invisible God and a brother of Christ, the Christian finds in every man God himself and God's absolute demand for justice and love." Synod of Bishops, *Justice in the World* (1971) 34.

5th Sunday in Ordinary Time

Readings: Isaiah 58:7-10
1 Corinthians 2:1-5
Matthew 5:13-16

In today's Gospel, Jesus tells us that we are the light of the world. *Your light must shine before men so that they may see goodness in your acts and give praise to your heavenly Father.*

The light that shines in us is a reflection of Jesus, who says of himself, *I am the light of the world.* If we are to be *a light in darkness*, it must come from our following Christ.

The first reading spells out the quality of the light that we bring to the world: *Share your bread with the hungry, shelter the oppressed and the homeless; clothe the naked when you see them ... then your light shall break forth like the dawn. The just man is a light in darkness* because *lavishly he gives to the poor.*

Hunger, oppression, homelessness and poverty are all different forms of darkness. It is a darkness, however, which can be overcome: *If you remove from your midst oppression,... if you bestow your bread on the hungry,... then light shall rise for you in the darkness, and the gloom shall become for you like midday.*

Father, watch over your family. May our human home become a place of light.

"Christ, to be sure, gave His Church no proper mission in the political, economic, or social order. The purpose which He set before her is a religious one. But out of this religious mission itself come a function, a light, and an energy which can serve to structure and consolidate the human community according to the divine law." Vatican II, *Constitution on the Church in the Modern World* (1965) 42.

6th Sunday in Ordinary Time

Readings: Sirach 15:15-20
1 Corinthians 2:6-10
Matthew 5:17-37

The focus of today's liturgy is *obedience to God's word.* We are challenged to *keep the commandments,* to *walk in the law of the Lord.*

In order to keep the commandments, we must first know what they are and then we must understand them correctly. Jesus deals with this problem in the Gospel. The Jews had a law about murder, but they had misread it to mean that one was in the clear as long as one was not actually, personally killing someone. Jesus challenged his Jewish followers to follow the correct interpretation of the law, which meant that they were not to be the kind of people who would kill or would do anything that leads to someone else's death.

We Christians believe that God's *command of perfect love* obliges us to *do what is just and right.* It is not good enough to stay out of trouble; we must work at setting things right in the world. It is not good enough to give food to the hungry; we must work at making ours a society in which people do not go hungry.

Give me discernment, that I may observe your law and keep it with all my heart.

"The responsibility for alleviating the plight of the poor falls upon all members of society. As individuals, all citizens have a duty to assist the poor through acts of charity and personal commitment. But private charity and voluntary action are not sufficient. We also carry out our moral responsibility to assist and empower the poor by working collectively through government to establish just and effective public policies." U.S. Bishops, *Economic Justice for All* (1986) 189.

7th Sunday in Ordinary Time

Readings: Leviticus 19:1-2, 17-18
1 Corinthians 3:16-23
Matthew 5:38-48

An eye for an eye, a tooth for a tooth is one of the most quoted, and most misquoted, passages of the Bible. It does not represent the final biblical word, which is a message of forgiveness and ending the cycle of violence. *Take no revenge and cherish no grudge*, the reading from Leviticus tells us. *When a person strikes you on the right cheek, turn and offer him the other*, the Gospel says.

Perhaps the clearest indication that this is a difficult message to accept is the widespread support for the death penalty, even among people who claim to be followers of the one who told us to turn the other cheek. It isn't easy, this business of loving your enemies and praying for your persecutors. The world scoffs at such foolishness, but Paul makes it clear that we are to choose the foolishness of the Gospel over the wisdom of the world: *If any one of you thinks he is wise in a worldly way, he had better become a fool.*

Actually, it's not so much a matter of foolishness as it is a matter of holiness: *Be holy, for I, the Lord, your God, am holy.* It may be foolish to forgive, but it is unholy to seek revenge. The choice we face is between unholiness and a different kind of wisdom.

"We urge our brothers and sisters in Christ to remember the teaching of Jesus, who called us to be reconciled with those who have injured us (Mt 5:43-45) and to pray for forgiveness for our sins 'as we forgive those who have sinned against us' (Mt 6:12). We call on you to contemplate the crucified Christ, who set us the supreme example of forgiveness and of the triumph of compassionate love." U.S. Bishops, *Statement on Capital Punishment* (1980) 23.

8th Sunday in Ordinary Time

Readings: Isaiah 49:14-15
1 Corinthians 4:1-5
Matthew 6:24-34

The Sermon on the Mount contains teachings that are hard to swallow, such as the one in today's Gospel: *do not worry about your livelihood, what you are to eat or drink or use for clothing.* Did Jesus really mean that I am not to be concerned about my personal well-being?

Yes, he did. My attitude toward my own personal well-being should be one of trust. *Rest in God alone; trust in him at all times.* God's self-revelation has presented us with a challenge to let go, to trust totally in God's maternal care. *Can a mother forget her infant, be without tenderness for the child of her womb? Even should she forget, I will never forget you.*

The teaching of Jesus is clear. His followers concern themselves with the well-being of others, worrying about what others will eat and how others will clothe themselves. As for their own well-being, they place all their hope in God and they *stop worrying over questions like, "What are we to eat, or what are we to drink, or what are we to wear?"*

"The sordid love of wealth, which is the shame and great sin of our age, will be opposed in actual fact by the gentle yet effective law of Christian moderation which commands men to seek first the Kingdom of God and his justice, with the assurance that, by virtue of God's kindness and unfailing promise, temporal goods also, in so far as he has need of them, shall be given him besides." Pope Pius XI, *Quadragesimo Anno* (1931) 136.

9th Sunday in Ordinary Time

Readings: Deuteronomy 11:18, 26-28
Romans 3:21-25, 28
Matthew 7:21-27

There are many words competing for our attention. There are the words of politicians promising us all the things they think we want. There are the words of advertisers telling us to find happiness in buying the latest products. There are the words of the dominant culture telling us the socially correct way to think and act. Not all these words are bad, but to base one's life on them *is like the foolish man who built his house on sandy ground. The rains fell, the torrents came, the winds blew and lashed against his house. It collapsed under all this and was completely ruined.*

There is also the Word of God telling us to put God first, to care for others at least as much as we care for ourselves, and to live lives of service to all our brothers and sisters in need. *A blessing* awaits us *for obeying the commandments of the Lord,* and whoever bases his life on the Word of God *is like the wise man who built his house on rock. When the rainy season set in, the torrents came and the winds blew and buffeted his house. It did not collapse; it had been solidly set on rock.*

"In the sacred books, the Father who is in heaven meets his children with great love and speaks with them; and the force and power in the word of God is so great that it remains the support and energy of the Church, the strength of faith for her sons, the food of the soul, the pure and perennial source of spiritual life."
Vatican II, *Constitution on Divine Revelation* (1965) 21.

LENT

1st Sunday of Lent

Readings: Genesis 2:7-9; 3:1-7
Romans 5:12-19
Matthew 4:1-11

Jesus went into the wilderness and struggled with the demons. Such is the metaphor of spiritual life presented to us in today's Gospel. In the course of our lives, we are all *led into the desert by the Spirit*, and we must struggle with the demons.

We struggle with the demon of self-sufficiency. Ignoring our interdependence, we imagine that we can 'go it alone,' and end up dividing ourselves into isolated units of races, classes, and genders, living as though we do not need the other. We may even reach the point of living as though we do not need the Other.

We struggle with the demon of power. We begin by setting ourselves above others, and often end with oppressing them, using our power in a cruel or unjust manner to keep others down.

We struggle with the demon of pride, imagining ourselves to be better than others, or the 'top dog' in our little world, or number one in the world.

Lent is a time to struggle with the demons, *to rid ourselves of the hidden corruption of evil.*

Be merciful, O Lord, for we have sinned.

"As the kernel and center of his good news, Christ proclaims salvation, this great gift of God which is liberation from everything that oppresses man but which is above all liberation from sin and the evil one, in the joy of knowing God and being known by him, of seeing him, and of being given over to him." Pope Paul VI, *Evangelii Nuntiandi* (1975) 9.

2nd Sunday of Lent

Readings: Genesis 12:1-4
2 Timothy 1:8-10
Matthew 17:1-9

High on the mountain, the three disciples witness a dazzling sight as Jesus is transfigured before their eyes, his face as bright as the sun and his clothes as radiant as light. In the middle of this vision, they hear God's voice telling them to listen to *my beloved Son on whom my favor rests.* The opening prayer focuses our attention on this part of the story: *God our Father, help us to hear your Son.* The verse before the Gospel does the same: *From the shining cloud the Father's voice is heard: this is my beloved Son; hear him.*

Lent is a time to listen to Jesus, *who calls us to repentance and a change of heart.* It is a time to reflect on God's Word about loving our enemies and being peacemakers, about proclaiming liberty to captives and letting the oppressed go free, about being the salt of the earth and the light of the world, about being perfect just as our heavenly Father is perfect. It is a time to be quiet and listen to the God who *has saved us and has called us to a holy life.* It is a time to become *a great nation* through whom *all the communities of the earth shall find blessing.*

"Jesus perfected revelation by fulfilling it through his whole work of making himself present and manifesting himself: through his words and deeds, his signs and wonders, but especially through his death and glorious resurrection from the dead and final sending of the Spirit of truth. Moreover, he confirmed with divine testimony what revelation proclaimed: that God is with us to free us from the darkness of sin and death, and to raise us up to life eternal." Vatican II, *Constitution on Divine Revelation* (1965) 4.

3rd Sunday of Lent

Readings: Exodus 17:3-7
Romans 5:1-2, 5-8
John 4:5-42

In today's Gospel, Jesus promises the Samaritan woman *living water* which *shall become a fountain within her, leaping up to provide eternal life*. The liturgy on this Lenten Sunday places Jesus' promise within the context of the Exodus account of water coming from the rock of Horeb. The responsorial psalm 95 refers both to *the Rock of our salvation* and also to hardened hearts. On the one hand, there is the Rock (God) from which the water of eternal life flows. On the other hand, there are those rocks (our hearts) which we seek in Lent to soften *by prayer, fasting and works of mercy*.

We believe, with Paul, that *the love of God has been poured out in our hearts through the Holy Spirit*. That love of God should make us a forgiving people, one that enables the world to *be brought together in unity and peace*. Our goal is to *harden not our hearts*: to be concerned for the poor and suffering, to forgive the criminal, to welcome the stranger, to love our enemies.

If only you recognized God's gift ...

"By becoming for people a model of merciful love for others, Christ proclaims by his actions even more than by his words that call to mercy which is one of the essential elements of the gospel *ethos*. In this instance it is not just a case of fulfilling a commandment or an obligation of an ethical nature: it is also a case of satisfying a condition of major importance for God to reveal himself in his mercy to man: 'The merciful ... shall obtain mercy.'"
Pope John Paul II, *Dives in Misericordia* (1980) 3.

4th Sunday of Lent

Readings: 1 Samuel 16:1, 6-7, 10-13
Ephesians 5:8-14
John 9:1-41

The prophet Samuel comes to Bethlehem to choose a new king from the family of Jesse. He rejects Jesse's oldest son because *Not as man sees does God see, because man sees the appearance but the Lord looks into the heart.* With this single statement, the Word of God unmasks much of the world's blindness. We look at poor people and see nothing other than rundown houses and littered streets. We look at the homeless and see nothing other than dirty faces and ragged clothes. We look at people who are different from us and we see nothing other than the color of their skin or the way they manipulate their bodily limbs.

In today's Gospel, Jesus, the light of the world, takes away the man's blindness. This wonderful story challenges us to *live as children of light.* Our Lenten prayer and sacrifice should serve to take away our blindness so that we can look into the hearts of others and love them as brothers and sisters. It should *turn hatred to love, conflict to peace, death to eternal life.* It should enable us to say with the blind man: I can see and I believe in God.

"God's word proclaims the oneness of the human family—from the first words of Genesis, to the 'Come, Lord Jesus' of the Book of Revelation. God's word in Genesis announces that all men and women are created in God's image; not just some races and racial types, but all bear the imprint of the Creator and are enlivened by the breath of his one Spirit." U.S. Bishops, *Brothers and Sisters to Us* (1979) 25.

5th Sunday of Lent

Readings: Ezekiel 37:12-14
Romans 8:8-11
John 11:1-45

Today's Gospel recounts one of the most dramatic stories from the life of Jesus: the raising of Lazarus from the dead. John goes to great lengths to make clear that Lazarus had been dead for some time, and he shows Jesus' power to conquer death.

We live in a world that has been caught up in death for a long time. We kill each other in acts of murder, abortion, euthanasia, execution, war, terrorist activities, drunk and reckless driving. We kill ourselves through suicide, drug and alcohol abuse, smoking, overwork, stress, bad eating habits, and physical neglect. We watch calmly as others die from poverty, hunger and malnutrition, homelessness, unemployment, poor education, disease, lack of health coverage, child abuse, arms proliferation, discrimination, pollution, destruction of the environment, unsafe working conditions, and all the laws, policies, practices and attitudes which contribute to these conditions.

Jesus is the resurrection and the life. He is the God who *will put my spirit in you that you may live.* Our Lenten celebration must serve to remind us that the paschal mystery represents a victory over death.

"The right to life ... is basic and inalienable. It is grievously violated in our day by abortion and euthanasia, by widespread torture, by acts of violence against innocent parties, and by the scourge of war. The arms race is an insanity which burdens the world and creates the conditions for even more massive destruction of life." Pope Paul VI, *Message Issued in Union with the Synod of Bishops* (1974).

Passion Sunday (Palm Sunday)

Readings: Isaiah 50:4-7
Philippians 2:6-11
Matthew 26:14-27

Today we celebrate Jesus, the suffering Messiah. He is the one of whom Isaiah foretold: *My face I did not shield from buffets and spitting.* He is the Christ who *took the form of a slave,... obediently accepting even death, death on a cross.* He is the savior who *suffered willingly for sinners* and whose suffering makes us pleasing to God.

We all suffer in our own way. We experience physical pain and hardship. We suffer watching our friends and relatives suffer. We are often offended or abandoned by others, and we add to our suffering by our own sinfulness.

The world around us is filled with suffering: the victims of war and poverty; people living in streets or in shantytowns; starving children; lonely elderly; people dying of AIDS, cancer, or some other disease.

Today's liturgy teaches us to welcome our suffering, *to bear witness to (God) by following (Christ's) example of suffering.* We pray that the world *united with him in his suffering on the cross* may *share his resurrection and new life.*

"Had Jesus merely said that his mission was to set people free from sin and all forms of oppression, his words would have fallen on deaf ears. He had to work at this task of liberation. He not only talked about freeing the poor and oppressed but, undeterred by criticism, actually welcomed the poor and sinners to share at his table. Like Jesus, we must be able to accompany others in their suffering and be willing to suffer with them." U.S. Bishops, *To the Ends of the Earth* (1986) 48.

EASTER

Easter Sunday

Readings: Acts 10:34, 37-43
Colossians 3:1-4/1 Corinthians 5:6-8
John 20:1-9/Mark 16:1-8

This is the day the Lord has made; let us rejoice and be glad. Easter is the great celebration of victory of life over death.

Ours is an Easter religion. We do not deny or turn away from the evils that surround us: the wars that have killed some 100 million people in our century; the poverty that grips more than half of the human race; the hunger that kills millions every year and ruins the lives of millions more; the discrimination that divides the human family into contending parties. We do not deny these miseries, but we refuse to surrender to their power because of our faith in the resurrection of Jesus Christ. Suffering will be vindicated; death will be overcome; a new life will arise: that is the Easter message of the paschal mystery.

Let us feast with joy in the Lord. Just as Christ passed through death to resurrection, so too will the world pass through its suffering to the glory of a new life. There is no room for despair: our Easter faith tells us that God will *raise us up and renew our lives.*

"This is the 'day which the Lord has made.' Alleluia! Take fresh hope, brothers and sisters of the whole world! With Christ our Passover everything is possible! Christ goes forward in our future!" Pope John Paul II, Easter Message (1991) 8.

2nd Sunday of Easter

Readings: Acts 2:42-47
1 Peter 1:3-9
John 20:19-31

Jesus had been abandoned by his disciples at the time of his death. One of them had turned him over to the authorities. Another had denied he even knew Jesus. The others ran away, apparently in fear and horror.

That same fear still gripped the disciples as they stayed behind locked doors. The risen Jesus suddenly appeared among them, and there was not a word about their betrayal, denial, and abandonment. *Peace be with you*, he said, as though nothing had ever happened. They looked at his wounds, and he repeated his remarkable greeting: *Peace be with you*.

If only we could follow in the footsteps of Christ and wish peace to everyone! If only we could forgive as he forgave! Where would be the wars? the discrimination? the hatred? the death penalty? They would go the way of death itself, conquered by the resurrection.

Jesus assures us that we have received the Holy Spirit. We have the power to release others of their wrongs against us, just as we have the power to keep them and ourselves bound. Our Easter faith that *we have become a new creation* should strengthen our resolve to forgive as Christ forgave.

"We urge our brothers and sisters in Christ to remember the teaching of Jesus, who called us to be reconciled with those who have injured us and to pray for forgiveness for our sins 'as we forgive those who have sinned against us.' We call on you to contemplate the crucified Christ, who set us the supreme example of forgiveness and of the triumph of compassionate love." U.S. Bishops, *Statement on Capital Punishment* (1980) 23.

3rd Sunday of Easter

Readings: Acts 2:14, 22-28
1 Peter 1:17-21
Luke 24:13-35

The two disciples are leaving Jerusalem. They had been caught up in the experience of following Jesus, and they were devastated by his crucifixion. Moreover, they were undoubtedly frightened by the prospect of what might happen to them as followers of the executed master.

On their way from Jerusalem to Emmaus, they have an unusual encounter. The man they find themselves walking with seems to understand much about the scriptures, but they aren't able to make the connection between what he says and who he is. It is only in welcoming him into their house and sharing a meal with him that they realize who it is they are facing: it is Jesus, the risen Lord. So moved are they by the encounter that they turn around and head back to Jerusalem, to join up with the other disciples but also to face risk and uncertainty. They may very well have headed straight into martyrdom.

The Easter event can also turn around our lives. It can cause us to *rise and come forth into the light of day*, but we must be prepared for the risk and uncertainty such a conversion would entail.

"For the Church, evangelizing means bringing the good news into all the strata of humanity, and through its influence transforming humanity from within and making it new.... The purpose of evangelization is (an) interior change, and if it has to be expressed in one sentence the best way of stating it would be to say that the Church evangelizes when she seeks to convert, solely through the divine power of the message she proclaims, both the personal and collective consciences of people, the activities in which they engage, and the lives and concrete milieux which are theirs." Pope Paul VI, *Evangelii Nuntiandi* (1975) 18.

4th Sunday of Easter

Readings: Acts 2:14, 36-41
1 Peter 2:20-25
John 10:1-10

The risen Jesus is the true shepherd, *the one who enters through the gate*, who *walks in front of them, and the sheep follow him because they recognize his voice.*

True Christians follow the true shepherd: they recognize his voice and they obey his commands. They hear his message about loving enemies, about seeking first the kingdom of God, about forgiving seventy times a day. They hear him talk of concern for the poor, of selling all that one has, of being perfect as their heavenly Father is perfect. They listen to him say that they should not worry about tomorrow, that they should turn the other cheek, that they should lose their lives. They hear and obey, following their shepherd through the gate.

There are false shepherds who speak other words, who talk of defending one's rights, of accumulating wealth, of achieving social prominence. Some Christians listen to them rather than to the true shepherd.

Both the true and the false shepherds lead one to death. The difference is that the true shepherd leads beyond death to resurrection.

"In Christ and through Christ God has revealed himself fully to mankind and has definitively drawn close to it; at the same time, in Christ and through Christ man has acquired full awareness of his dignity, of the heights to which he is raised, of the surpassing worth of his own humanity, and of the meaning of his existence." Pope John Paul II, *Redemptor Hominis* (1979) 11.

5th Sunday of Easter

Readings: Acts 6:1-7
1 Peter 2:4-9
John 14:1-12

The risen Jesus is *the way, and the truth, and the life.*
Jesus is the way, the path to eternal life with the Father: *no one comes to the Father but through me.* To try another way is to ensure failure.
Jesus is the truth, the word of God. To seek the truth elsewhere is to *stumble and fall,* to deal in falsehood and lie.
Jesus is the life, the God who has *filled all ages with the words of a new song.* To live outside of Christ is to die.
Those who follow Jesus faithfully are *a chosen race, a royal priesthood, a consecrated nation.* They are chosen to *proclaim the glorious works* of God. They are priestly mediators *offering spiritual sacrifices acceptable to God.* They are consecrated to *the One who called you from darkness.* Built on the cornerstone of Jesus Christ, they are a powerful community, descending from that early church where *the word of God continued to spread* and *the number of disciples ... enormously increased.*

"When Jesus rose up again after suffering death on the cross for mankind, He manifested that He had been appointed Lord, Messiah, and Priest forever, and He poured out on His disciples the Spirit promised by the Father. The Church, consequently, equipped with the gifts of her Founder and faithfully guarding His precepts of charity, humility, and self-sacrifice, receives the mission to proclaim and to establish among all peoples the kingdom of Christ and of God." Vatican II, *Constitution on the Church* (1964) 5.

6th Sunday of Easter

Readings: Acts 8:5-8, 14-17
1 Peter 3:15-18
John 14:15-21

In today's Gospel Jesus promises us that *I will not leave you orphaned; I will come back to you* and *you will have life.* Our faith, nurtured in this great paschal season, tells us that God-made-flesh is God-with-us, never abandoning us and always filling us with life.

It should be a great comfort to all of us, who share in the pain and suffering of ordinary life, to know that the Spirit of Jesus is with us always. It should be especially comforting to know that Jesus will not leave orphaned all those whom the world casts aside: the poor and homeless, the racial and ethnic minorities, the sick and dying, the prisoner and the refugee.

Christ died for sins once for all, a just man for the sake of the unjust. He rescued us from our attachment to injustice, and then he sent his Spirit to remain with us and within us. Our prayer is one of gratitude for such a gift and hope that *we feel its saving power in our daily life.*

"Jesus loves us so much that, even after his death, resurrection, and ascension, he remains with us. He is, after all, Emanuel, 'God with us,' but now through his living, sanctifying Spirit. We now encounter him in new ways: in other human beings; in any place where people gather in his name; in the inspired words of Holy Scripture; in his Church, particularly her liturgical celebrations; in the person of his minister; and especially in the sacraments." U.S. Bishops, *The Eucharist and the Hungers of the Human Family* (1975) 7.

7th Sunday of Easter

Readings: Acts 1:12-14
1 Peter 4:13-16
John 17:1-11

Having ascended into heaven, Jesus can now say that *I am in the world no more, but these are in the world.* He is not physically present in the world the way he was in the first third of the first century. It is now up to us to deal with the world.

During the period dominated by Trent and Vatican I, the Catholic Church was defensive in its approach to the world, which was regarded as an occasion of sin. Vatican II heralded a new approach based on dialogue rather than confrontation. The world is viewed not as the enemy but rather as the object of service. This positive approach is much closer to our biblical roots: *I believe that I shall see the good things of the Lord in the land of the living.*

Time is the unfolding of truth that already is. The world and its history are where we encounter the eternal God, *reaching from end to end of the universe.* We are not called to abandon the world but to remain in it and to take responsibility for its well ordering. The paschal mystery is a challenge to us to lift the world to the heavens.

"Holding faithfully to the gospel and exercising her mission in the world, the Church consolidates peace among men, to God's glory. For it is her task to uncover, cherish, and ennoble all that is true, good, and beautiful in the human community." Vatican II, *Constitution on the Church in the Modern World* (1965) 76.

Pentecost

Readings: Acts 2:1-11
1 Corinthians 12:3-7, 12-13
John 20:19-23

Thus says the Lord: I will pour out my spirit upon all mankind. Your sons and daughters shall prophesy, your old men shall see visions.

The coming of the Spirit should fill us with dreams and visions of a better world. Let us dream in the Spirit of a classless society in which all people are regarded and treated as equals. Let us dream in the Spirit of a nonviolent world in which there is no war, no terrorist attacks on innocent people, no murder, and no death penalty. Let us dream in the Spirit of a world of economic justice in which all people have their basic needs met, and no one lives in poverty, hunger, or homelessness. Let us dream in the Spirit of a world of love, forgiveness, and service.

Lord, send out your Spirit, and renew the face of the earth. May the Spirit of God guide us to end the suffering we have brought on ourselves and *unite the faces and nations on earth to proclaim your glory.*

"The People of God believes that it is led by the Spirit of the Lord, who fills the earth. Motivated by this faith, it labors to decipher authentic signs of God's presence and purpose in the happenings, needs, and desires in which this People has a part along with other men of our age. For faith throws a new light on everything, manifests God's design for man's total vocation, and thus directs the mind to solutions which are fully human." Vatican II, *Constitution on the Church in the Modern World* (1965) 11.

ORDINARY TIME AFTER PENTECOST

Trinity Sunday

Readings: Exodus 34:4-6, 8-9
2 Corinthians 13:11-13
John 3:16-18

One of the foundational truths of our faith is the *one God in three Persons*: *Father all-powerful, Christ Lord and Savior, Spirit of love*. We can reason our way into knowledge of the existence of God, but we would never know of God as Trinity if it were not revealed to us.

There is much else about God that has been revealed: about God as giver of life, land, and food; about God as liberator and protector; about the God of peace and the God of covenant love; about the suffering God, the God of the poor; about the God made flesh, the God with us. None of this comes from reason, although it does not contradict reason. Most of what we know about God we know because God has revealed it to us.

On this Trinity Sunday, it would be good to reflect on the God of our faith and worship. Do we honor the God of revelation, or do we honor a god of our own making? Do we honor the vengeful god of a merciless world, or do we honor *the Lord, a merciful and gracious God, slow to anger and rich in kindness and fidelity*?

"In his goodness and wisdom, God chose to reveal himself and to make known to us the hidden purpose of his will by which through Christ, the Word made flesh, man has access to the Father in the Holy Spirit and comes to share in the divine nature. Through this revelation, therefore, the invisible God out of the abundance of his love speaks to men as friends and lives among them, so that he may invite and take them into fellowship with himself." Vatican II, *Constitution on Divine Revelation* (1965) 2.

The Body and Blood of Christ (Corpus Christi)

Readings: Deuteronomy 8:2-3, 14-16
1 Corinthians 10:16-17
John 6:51-58

We celebrate the body and blood of Christ not as isolated objects of adoration but as food and drink, like the manna in the desert and the water brought forth from a rock. Jesus makes it very clear how we are to approach his body and blood: *if you do not eat the flesh of the Son of Man and drink his blood you have no life in you. He who feeds on my flesh and drinks my blood has life eternal.*

The food that we eat every day, and the liquids we drink, become part of our bodies, sustaining them and allowing them to grow, function, and heal. The food that is the body and blood of Christ does something far greater; it makes us one with God. *The man who feeds on my flesh and drinks my blood remains in me, and I in him.* This is why the body and blood of Christ signify unity and peace: there is one Christ, and all who eat and drink the body and blood of Christ become one in the one Christ. *We, many though we are, are one body, for we all partake of the one loaf.* There is no room for disunity among those who eat and drink the body and blood of Christ.

"The mysterious reality of the Eucharist—'My flesh is real food and my blood real drink' (Jn 6:55)—is a puzzle to some, a scandal to others. It has always been so.... But for those who believe in Jesus' teaching because they believe in Jesus Christ himself, the Eucharist is, among all his gifts to us, the most cherished and the cause of our deepest gratitude." U.S. Bishops, *The Eucharist and the Hungers of the Human Family* (1975) 18-19.

10th Sunday in Ordinary Time

Readings: Hosea 6:3-6
Romans 4:18-25
Matthew 9:9-13

The prophet Hosea declared on behalf of God: *It is love that I desire, not sacrifice.* In Matthew's gospel Jesus quotes this a little differently: *It is mercy I desire, and not sacrifice.* In either case, the message is the same: God is less interested in our specifically religious practices and more interested in the way we treat others. Perhaps it is better to say that religious practices are pleasing to God when they reflect the lives of people who are in right relationship to other people.

The problem with so many of us that our *piety is like a morning cloud, like the dew that early passes away.* We do not love as Christ teaches. We see Jesus *eating with tax collectors and those who disregard the law*, but when he tells us *Follow me*, we hesitate because it is hard to mix with the outcasts of the world. It is, after all, the Christian majority in our country which isolates the homeless, pours contempt on the poor, and legislates into existence those death rows which house the kind of sinners Jesus said he came to call.

Words cannot measure the boundaries of love for those born to new life in Christ Jesus. We need to expand the boundaries of our response to that love.

"The option or love of preference for the poor... is an option, or a special form of primacy in the exercise of Christian charity, to which the whole tradition of the Church bears witness. It affects the life of each Christian inasmuch as he or she seeks to imitate the life of Christ, but it applies equally to our social responsibilities and hence to our manner of living, and to the logical decisions to be made concerning the ownership and use of goods." Pope John Paul II, *Sollicitudo Rei Socialis* (1987) 42.

11th Sunday in Ordinary Time

Readings: Exodus 19:2-6
Romans 5:6-11
Matthew 9:36—10:8

Jesus chose twelve apostles, and then he sent them out to do work. This work was not religious in the sense of leading people to prayer and good works, but it was very religious nonetheless. The apostles were charged with changing people's lives, removing the obstacles that kept people from living full lives. They were told to *cure the sick, raise the dead, heal the leprous, expel demons.* Their task, in other words, was to make a difference in people's lives.

What difference does our practice of Christianity make in the lives of people? Are the suffering and dying better off because we follow Christ? Are the hungry and homeless finding their lives improved because we follow Christ? Do children have a brighter future because we follow Christ?

God tells us that *you shall be my special possession, dearer to me than all other people.* Surely this does not mean that God does not love all those others. We are dearer to God for reasons unknown to us, and there can be no doubt that we have a mission to be *a kingdom of priests,* mediators between suffering humanity and the God who is *our hope and our strength.*

"In all its activities the Church must seek to preach and act in ways that lead to greater justice for all people. Its ministry cannot neglect the violations of human rights resulting from racism, poverty, poor housing, inadequate education and health care, widespread apathy and indifference, and a lack of freedom. These realities are fundamentally incompatible with our faith, and the Church is required to oppose them." U.S. Bishops, *Statement on American Indians* (1977) 10.

12th Sunday in Ordinary Time

Readings: Jeremiah 20:10-13
Romans 5:12-15
Matthew 10:26-33

God is the strength of his people, the *guide and protector of your people*, the one who keeps us secure *from this world's uncertainty*. We should *not be afraid of anything* because *the Lord is with me, like a mighty champion*.

The poor and lowly are special objects of protection. *See, you lowly ones, and be glad ... for the Lord hears the poor, for he has rescued the life of the poor*. The special care of the poor is a sign to all of us that God is our strength, for it means that God is not influenced by the judgments of the world. The world might abuse and ignore the poor and lowly, but God hears their cry and rescues their lives. The riches of this world might be for a select few, the rich and powerful, but *the gracious gift of Jesus Christ abounds for all*.

So *do not let men intimidate you*. Our God is God of the poor and lowly, and *in him, we his children live in safety*.

"In the Old Testament God reveals himself to us as the liberator of the oppressed and the defender of the poor, demanding from man faith in him and justice towards man's neighbor. It is only in the observance of the duties of justice that God is truly recognized as the liberator of the oppressed." Synod of Bishops, *Justice in the World* (1971) 30.

13th Sunday in Ordinary Time

Readings: 2 Kings 4:8-11, 14-16
Romans 6:3-4, 8-11
Matthew 10:37-42

The prophet Elisha is welcomed warmly by the couple in Shunem, and he promises them a reward for their hospitality. Jesus tells his followers that *he who welcomes you welcomes me, and he who welcomes me welcomes him who sent me.*

How good are we as a society at welcoming people into our company? An asylum underground operated during the 1980s to give protection to Salvadorans and Guatemalans whom we did not want to welcome. The Haitians have not been so lucky in the 1990s. The homeless are often not welcome anywhere, locked outside by a society that does not want to adequately fund public housing and pursued by the enforcers of laws that make it illegal to be homeless. Stories continue to surface of high-class institutions refusing to welcome African Americans or Jews or women.

Those of us who are baptized *must consider ourselves dead to sin but alive for God in Christ Jesus.* We should *walk in the light of Christ.* We should be different from those who exclude others and drive them out. We should *bring God's love to the world.*

"Basic justice demands the establishment of minimum levels of participation in the life of the human community for all persons ... The ultimate injustice is for a person or group to be treated actively or abandoned passively as if they were nonmembers of the human race. To treat people this way is effectively to say that they simply do not count as human beings." U.S. Bishops, *Economic Justice for All* (1986) 77.

14th Sunday in Ordinary Time

Readings: Zechariah 9:9-10
Romans 8:9, 11-13
Matthew 11:25-30

The world looks for strength in power, the ability to control others. It looks for strength in wealth, the ability to own and accumulate possessions. It looks for strength in developing advantages over others, such as superior education and prestigious positions.

Revelation presents a different picture. It introduces us to a messiah who is *meek, and riding on an ass*. It wants us to believe that our strength is in a man whose boast is that *I am gentle and humble of heart*. It praises God for contradicting the wisdom of the world: *for what you have hidden from the learned and the clever you have revealed to the merest children*.

Maybe we continue to suffer so many miseries because we look for answers in the wrong places. We look "up" at the rich and powerful, expecting to find strength and security, and we are disillusioned with *empty promises of passing joy*. Perhaps we should look "down" at the meek and humble, the little people, the sick and dying, the poor and hungry. For it is among them that we will find our *just savior*, the God whose *right hand is filled with justice*.

"The power of the Spirit, who raised Christ from the dead, is continuously at work in the world. Through the generous sons and daughters of the Church likewise, the people of God is present in the midst of the poor and of those who suffer oppression and persecution; it lives in its own flesh and its own heart the Passion of Christ and bears witness to his resurrection." Synod of Bishops, *Justice in the World* (1971) 74.

15th Sunday in Ordinary Time

Readings: Isaiah 55:10-11
Romans 8:18-23
Matthew 13:1-23

The parable of the sower is a story about the fruitfulness of the earth. It assures us that the harvest will come in spite of the many obstacles that stand in the way. In the end, the rocks and birds and trampling feet cannot nullify the fact that *the seed that falls on good ground will yield a fruitful harvest.*

Paul talks about the salvation of the world, pointing out that *the world itself will be freed from its slavery to corruption and share in the glorious freedom of the children of God.* Meanwhile, *all creation groans and is in agony*: we pollute the clear air and the fresh water; we drive plants and animals to extinction; we clear-cut forests and we strip-mine, leaving ugly scars in the land.

The opening prayer calls on us to *reject what is contrary to the gospel.* Isn't it contrary to the "good news" to waste and destroy God's creation? The Creator has *greatly enriched the land.* How dare we impoverish it!

"The commitment of believers to a healthy environment for everyone stems directly from their belief in God the Creator, from their recognition of the effects of original and personal sin, and from the certainty of having been redeemed by Christ. Respect for life and for the dignity of the human person extends also to the rest of creation, which is called to join man in praising God." Pope John Paul II, World Day of Peace Message (1990) 16.

16th Sunday in Ordinary Time

Readings: Wisdom 12:13, 16-19
Romans 8:26-27
Matthew 13:24-43

Matthew is very concerned in his Gospel with the unity of the Christian community. He does not envision the Church as an exclusive club, but rather as an inclusive community which is guided by the spirit of the parable of the weeds. *Let them grow together until harvest*: since its earliest days, the Church has preferred to tolerate different levels of commitment and holiness. Such an attitude is in line with the 'wisdom' of the Hebrew Scriptures, which informs us that *those who are just must be kind* and *your mastery over all things makes you lenient to all* and *you judge with clemency*. This attitude of acceptance is also in line with the revelation of God as *merciful and gracious, slow to anger, abounding in kindness.*

An inclusive Church that is kind and lenient toward its own members and toward everyone else should be an inspiration to a divided world that has a tendency to judge harshly, to be quick to anger, and to uproot weeds even at the cost of damage to the good plants.

"By virtue of her mission to shed on the whole world the radiance of the gospel message, and to unify under one Spirit all men of whatever nation, race, or culture, the Church stands forth as a sign of that brotherliness which allows honest dialogue and invigorates it. Such a mission requires in the first place that we foster within the Church herself mutual esteem, reverence, and harmony, through the full recognition of lawful diversity." Vatican II, *Constitution on the Church in the Modern World* (1965) 92.

17th Sunday in Ordinary Time

Readings: 1 Kings 3:5, 7-12
Romans 8:28-30
Matthew 13:44-52

Jesus likens the kingdom to a man who finds a buried treasure and sells all that he has so that he can buy the field containing the treasure. He likens the kingdom to a merchant who sells all that he has in order to be able to buy *one really valuable pearl.*

What is the *one really valuable pearl* for which we are willing to sacrifice everything? What is that buried treasure for which we would be willing to sacrifice everything? The thing that Solomon wanted most was *an understanding heart to judge your people and to distinguish right from wrong.*

Isn't it possible that what we want most is something very selfish: possessions, security, power, pleasure, comfort. What would the world be like if, instead of these, our *one really valuable pearl* was something like world peace based on justice for all? or the development of a classless society based on respect for all and the priority of need over want? or the worship of God through prayer, service, and a preferential option for the poor?

What would the world be like? Jesus says it would be like the kingdom.

"The cross of Jesus Christ shows us the deficiency of other value systems. Jesus yielded up his life for us in perfect loving union with the Father's will, and this is the meaning of his life which also gives meaning to our lives as his followers. If we can acknowledge selfishness as folly and self-sacrifice as victory, if we can love enemies, be vulnerable to injustice and, in being so, still say that we have triumphed, then we shall have learned to live in Christ Jesus." U.S. Bishops, *To Live in Christ Jesus* (1976) 116.

18th Sunday in Ordinary Time

Readings: Isaiah 55:1-3
Romans 8:35, 37-39
Matthew 14:13-21

We live in a wonderful home created by God to provide us with all that we need. It is a world that we neither deserve nor earn: *All you who are thirsty, come to the water! You who have no money, come, receive grain and eat; come, without paying and without cost, drink wine and milk!* In the midst of this world, however, there are countless millions who go to bed hungry every night, not knowing if there will be food on the table the next day.

The hand of the Lord feeds us. It feeds us, however, through the common efforts of others: note that Jesus, when feeding the five thousand, passed out the food in the hands of the disciples. He did this, moreover, right after telling them *Give them something to eat yourselves.*

The problem in feeding the world's population is not with the productivity of God's earth. The problem lies with our lack of political will, our economic system biased in favor of the affluent, our militarism, and our tendency to blame the victims of social tragedies like hunger.

Forgive our sins and restore us to life. The first step in eliminating hunger should be a universal confession of wrongdoing.

"The nations that enjoy a sufficiency and abundance of everything may not overlook the plight of other nations whose citizens experience such domestic problems that they are all but overcome by poverty and hunger, and are not able to enjoy basic human rights.... We think it opportune to stress here what we have stated in another connection: 'We all share responsibility for the fact that populations are undernourished. Therefore, it is necessary to arouse a sense of responsibility in individuals and generally, especially among those more blessed with this world's goods.'"
Pope John XXIII, *Mater et Magistra* (1961) 157-58.

19th Sunday in Ordinary Time

Readings: 1 Kings 19:9, 11-13
Romans 9:1-5
Matthew 14:22-33

The God of revelation is a hidden and mysterious God. The disciples experienced this God on the Sea of Galilee: they were caught in a storm while Jesus was up on a mountain by himself praying. The Gospel says they were terrified when they saw him walking on the water.

Elijah thought he would experience God in a strong and heavy wind, or in an earthquake, or in a fire. Instead he found God in *a tiny whispering sound.*

We keep thinking that God will be found in the great and powerful, and we wonder why so many people seem never to find God. Our sights have to be lowered, so to speak, from the powerful to the powerless, from the rich to the poor, from the satisfied to the suffering, from the oppressors to the oppressed. We have to listen carefully for the tiny whispering sounds of alienation and powerlessness.

Lord, let us see your kindness. Let us see it in all the little people who follow you, carrying their crosses of daily sacrifice, suffering, humiliation, and victimization.

"Though in the Gospels and in the New Testament as a whole the offer of salvation is extended to all peoples, Jesus takes the side of those most in need, physically and spiritually. The example of Jesus ... calls for an emptying of self, both individually and corporately, that allows the Church to experience the power of God in the midst of poverty and powerlessness." U.S. Bishops, *Economic Justice for All* (1986) 52.

20th Sunday in Ordinary Time

Readings: Isaiah 56:1, 6-7
Romans 11:13-15, 19-32
Matthew 15:21-28

The Canaanite woman was all alone: she was a Gentile in a Jewish world and a woman in a man's world, and she was isolated because of her menstrual hemorrhaging. What makes her special is her determination: she turns to her advantage Jesus' statement about not giving food to the dogs.

There can be no doubt that God's *care extends beyond the boundaries of race and nation to the hearts of all who live*, and that God's house should become *a house of prayer for all peoples*. It is therefore fitting that we should pray that *the walls, which prejudice raises between us, crumble*. But we must realize that an end to prejudice will not come easily, and it will be overcome only by the determination of the victims of prejudice.

Woman, you have great faith! Jesus did not resist the determined woman; rather, he praised her determination. Those of us who work and pray for an end to prejudice must follow Jesus in praising the determination of those who are claiming their rights as human beings.

"It is obvious to everyone that women are now taking part in public life. This is happening more rapidly perhaps in nations with a Christian tradition, and more slowly, but broadly, among peoples who have inherited other traditions or cultures. Since women are becoming ever more conscious of their human dignity, they will not tolerate being treated as inanimate objects or mere instruments, but claim, both in domestic and in public life, the rights and duties that befit a human person." Pope John XXIII, *Pacem in Terris* (1963) 41.

21st Sunday in Ordinary Time

Readings: Isaiah 22:15, 19-23
Romans 11:33-36
Matthew 16:13-20

You are 'Rock,' and on this rock I will build my church, and the jaws of death shall not prevail against it. The Catholic Church has always looked upon today's Gospel as the cornerstone of the Petrine ministry, the special role played by the successor of Peter. Catholics believe that the Bishop of Rome exercises a special authority over the church.

Authority within the context of the People of God is a special kind of authority. The reading from Isaiah is about removal from office for abuse of authority and replacement by someone who *shall be a father*. The purpose of authority in the church, authority at any level, is not to control the lives of others but rather to *help us to seek the values that will bring us lasting joy in this changing world.*

Those with any authority in the church should reflect on their exercise of that authority, and those under authority should reflect on their attitude to the leaders of the church. All of us should join in praying that the Lord *grant peace and unity to your Church.*

"For the nurturing and constant growth of the People of God, the Lord instituted in His Church a variety of ministries, which work for the good of the whole body. For those ministers who are endowed with sacred power are servants of their brethren, so that all who are of the People of God, and therefore enjoy a true Christian dignity, can work toward a common goal freely and in an orderly way, and arrive at salvation." Vatican II, *Constitution on the Church* (1964) 18.

22nd Sunday in Ordinary Time

Readings: Jeremiah 20:7-9
Romans 12:1-2
Matthew 16:21-27

Peter knew that Jesus was the messiah awaited by God's people, but he did not understand that Jesus would be a suffering messiah. *God forbid that any such thing ever happen to you!* But it did happen to Jesus, and it happens to those who follow him: *If a man wishes to come after me, he must deny his very self (and) take up his cross.* Jeremiah had foretold the suffering of those who work for the coming of the kingdom: *All the day I am an object of laughter; everyone mocks me... The word of the Lord has brought me derision and reproach all the day.*

It is not easy, this business of following Christ. You work for peace, and people accuse you of being unpatriotic. You stand up for the poor, and people write you off as a naive dreamer. You work for nonviolent change, like Martin Luther King, or Ita Ford, or Archbishop Oscar Romero, and they shoot you. Meanwhile, you calmly go about your life, praying that God *fill our hearts with love* and *increase our faith.*

Do not conform yourselves to this age, Paul wrote to the Romans. We pay a price for such an approach, but we do so willingly because of our faith in the *promise of salvation.*

"The Church, like a pilgrim in a foreign land, presses forward amid the persecutions of the world and the consolations of God, announcing the cross and death of the Lord until he comes. By the power of the risen Lord, she is given strength to overcome patiently and lovingly the afflictions and hardships which assail her from within and without, and to show forth in the world the mystery of the Lord in a faithful though shadowed way, until at the last it will be revealed in total splendor." Vatican II, *Constitution on the Church* (1964) 8.

23rd Sunday in Ordinary Time

Readings: Ezekiel 33:7-9
Romans 13:8-10
Matthew 18:15-20

We are a church, an assembly of people gathered to do the work of God. This work brings us together around the table of the Lord and sends us out to renew the face of the earth.

The task that faces us in the world is awesome, and the obstacles are formidable. The only way we can succeed is by staying together, with Jesus in our midst, and our staying together must involve community efforts to correct our faults. When there is racism or sexism in our church, we must confront them and work to eliminate them. When economic injustice is found in our church institutions, we must speak out against it and work to eliminate it. When militarism makes its way into the fabric of our community, we must stand up for peace and proclaim the gospel message of nonviolent change.

Owe no debt to anyone except the debt that binds us to love one another. An essential component of that love should be the help we give each other in overcoming the shortcomings that get in the way of our becoming a universal sacrament of salvation.

"We must serve the Church and love her as she is, with a clear understanding of history, and humbly searching for the will of God who assists and guides her even when at times He permits human weakness to eclipse the purity of her features and the beauty of her action. It is this purity and beauty which we are endeavoring to discover and promote." Pope Paul VI, *Ecclesiam Suam* (1964) 49.

24th Sunday in Ordinary Time

Readings: Sirach 27:30—28:7
Romans 14:7-9
Matthew 18:21-35

Forgive your neighbor's injustice. How often must I forgive the brother who wrongs me? *Not seven times, I say, seventy times seven times.*

Some of the social ills that we struggle against result in part from the refusal of people to forgive. Wars are fought and innocent people are killed, maimed, or displaced because people cannot forgive their neighbors for their actions or those of their ancestors. Our own society shows its own refusal to forgive in its obsessive clinging to the death penalty.

The world of social evil stands in need of forgiveness. Those of us who are African-American are challenged by the gospel to forgive the slave masters of their ancestors as well as the racist descendants of those slave masters. Those of us who are women are challenged by the gospel to forgive the sexist men who have colluded, through action or inaction, in the creation and maintenance of a 'man's world.' The victims of war are challenged by the gospel to forgive all the militarists of the world.

The Lord is kind and merciful; slow to anger and rich in compassion. The challenge is for us to become like God, who is *our creator and guide.*

"Mercy in itself, as a perfection of the infinite God, is also infinite. Also infinite therefore and inexhaustible is the Father's readiness to receive the prodigal children who return to his home. Infinite are the readiness and power of forgiveness which flow continually from the marvelous value of the sacrifice of the Son. No human sin can prevail over this power or even limit it." Pope John Paul II, *Dives in Misericordia* (1980) 13.

25th Sunday in Ordinary Time

Readings: Isaiah 55:6-9
Philippians 1:20-24, 27
Matthew 20:1-16

The parable of the workers in the vineyard is rather startling. People who work an hour in the late afternoon are paid the same as those who work all day long. Obviously God doesn't think like we do. We think of justice in terms of what is fair, of what people deserve. So we would say that the people who worked longer deserved more. But God doesn't see it that way. God thinks of justice in terms of people's dignity, their right to a decent life. The people who came late had the same right to a decent life as those who had worked all day, so they are all treated equally. Nothing is taken from anyone, but all are treated in accord with their dignity, their right to a decent life. Such is God's justice.

My thoughts are not your thoughts, nor are your ways my ways, says the Lord. Perhaps we would have a better world if we were to adopt some of God's ways. After all, *the Lord is just in all his ways*, and that is something which cannot be said of all our ways.

Father, guide us according to your law of love. Free us from our law of vindictive justice.

"Biblical justice is more comprehensive than subsequent philosophical definitions. It is not concerned with a strict definition of rights and duties, but with the rightness of the human condition before God and within society. Nor is justice opposed to love; rather, it is both a manifestation of love and a condition for love to grow." U.S. Bishops, *Economic Justice for All* (1986) 39.

26th Sunday in Ordinary Time

Readings: Ezekiel 18:25-28
Philippians 2:1-11
Matthew 21:28-32

Two sons were asked to work in the vineyard of their father. One said he would do so, but he didn't. The other said he wouldn't, but he did. It was this second son who *did what the father wanted.*

God, our Father, invites us all to work in the vineyard, preparing the world for the coming of the kingdom. Some of us talk about the work that needs to be done, calling attention to the social ills that divide us: the poverty and hunger, the discrimination and oppression, the militarism and war. Others of us do something about these problems: challenging the systems that produce poverty and hunger, struggling to overcome discrimination and oppression, agitating for peace and an end to militarism.

The challenge of Jesus Christ is to look to others' interests rather than to one's own. It is to look beyond one's small world, which may be filled with satisfaction and fulfillment, to look out into that world where people suffer and die. And it is to go beyond talk and become involved in action for the transformation of the world.

Two sons were asked to work in the vineyard of their father. One of them did what the father wanted.

"It is not enough to recall principles, state intentions, point to crying injustices and utter prophetic denunciations; these words will lack real weight unless they are accompanied for each individual by a livelier awareness of personal responsibility and by effective action." Pope Paul VI, *Octagesimo Adveniens* (1971) 48.

27th Sunday in Ordinary Time

Readings: Isaiah 5:1-7
Philippians 4:6-9
Matthew 21:33-43

The church is the vineyard of the Lord. It has been placed by God *on a fertile hillside; he spaded it, cleared it of stones, and planted the choicest vines.* Unfortunately, what grows in this vineyard is often not a crop of grapes but wild fruit, of no use to the master. We have within our community a good share of selfishness, power grabbing, and shortsightedness. The very same social ills that we see in the world at large can be found right here within our own community: racism, sexism, economic injustice, and marginalization.

We pray that God *forgive our failings.* We hope that God will *take care of this vine, and protect what your right hand has planted.* The challenge is for us to become a true vineyard of the Lord, free of all the sinful conditions that we lament in the world. We work for the day when Christians will form a Christian community united in love and service.

Is it too much to hope for? No, it is not, as long as we maintain our faith in our God, who can *lead us to seek beyond our reach.*

"Although the Catholic Church has been endowed with all divinely revealed truth and with all means of grace, her members fail to live by them with all the fervor they should. As a result, the radiance of the Church's face shines less brightly in the eyes of our separated brethren and of the world at large, and the growth of God's kingdom is retarded. Every Catholic must therefore aim at Christian perfection and, each according to his station, play his part so that the Church ... may daily be more purified and renewed." Vatican II, *Decree on Ecumenism* (1964) 4.

28th Sunday in Ordinary Time

Readings: Isaiah 25:6-10
Philippians 4:12-14, 19-20
Matthew 22:1-14

The Lord of hosts will provide for all peoples a feast of rich food and choice wines, juicy, rich food and pure, choice wines ... he will destroy the veil that veils all peoples ... he will destroy death forever. The kingdom has been prepared, and it is coming. Jesus likened it to a wedding banquet to which the invited guests are summoned.

Of course, there are some who refuse to come. They prefer to remain mired in their oppressive attitudes, their discriminatory relationships with others, their violent approach to solving social problems. They prefer revenge to forgiveness. They prefer the superiority of some to the equality of all. They see victimization and blame the victims. They are the invited guests who are *unfit to come.*

There are those others, however, whose love for God expresses itself in eagerness to do good for others. They are the ones who *live in the house of the Lord,* preferring love, forgiveness and equality. They will welcome the coming of the kingdom with the cry: *let us rejoice and be glad that God has saved us!*

"Christians cannot yearn for anything more ardently than to serve the men of the modern world ever more generously and effectively. Therefore, holding faithfully to the gospel and benefiting from its resources, and united with every man who loves and practices justice, Christians have shouldered a gigantic task demanding fulfillment in this world. Concerning this task they must give a reckoning to Him who will judge every man on the last day." Vatican II, *Constitution on the Church in the Modern World* (1965) 93.

29th Sunday in Ordinary Time

Readings: Isaiah 45:1, 4-6
1 Thessalonians 1:1-5
Matthew 22:15-21

I am the Lord and there is no other, there is no God besides me. The god that we make of power, the domination of others and the exercise of control over their lives, is a false god. The god that we make of possessions, the accumulation of wealth far beyond that required for a dignified life, is a false god. The god that we make of pleasure and comfort, soothing our senses with physical satisfaction and enjoyment, is a false god. The god that we make of security, lulling us to sleep in the midst of a world filled with chaos and turmoil, is a false god.

Give to Caesar what is Caesar's, but give to God what is God's. What is God's is the only place as God, and so we *give the Lord glory and honor.* We who *belong to God the Father and the Lord Jesus Christ* know that *all the gods of the nations are things of naught,* and so we reject the false gods of power, possessions, pleasure, and security. We place all our hope in the *almighty and ever-living God* who is *our source of power and inspiration.*

"Since it has been entrusted to the Church to reveal the mystery of God, who is the ultimate goal of man, she opens up to man at the same time the meaning of his own existence, that is, the innermost truth about himself. The Church truly knows that only God, whom she serves, meets the deepest longings of the human heart, which is never fully satisfied by what this world has to offer." Vatican II, *Constitution on the Church in the Modern World* (1965) 41.

30th Sunday in Ordinary Time

Readings: Exodus 22:20-26
1 Thessalonians 1:5-10
Matthew 22:34-40

The greatest commandment is clear: *You shall love the Lord your God with your whole heart.* The second greatest commandment is equally clear: *You shall love your neighbor as yourself.* What is not clear, perhaps, is what these commandments mean. The juxtaposition of these two commandments, both chosen from the Hebrew Scriptures, would seem to clarify at least to some extent what it means to love God: one way we humans express our love for God is by loving our neighbor. Today's liturgy attempts to clarify the matter of loving one's neighbor by another juxtaposition, preceding the Gospel with the passage from Exodus about treating justly the most vulnerable people in society. The implication is that loving our neighbor means more than being kind to our friends and relatives, or to the person who lives next door. Loving one's neighbor means doing right by *any widow or orphan*: seeing that the hungry are fed and the homeless sheltered, that the poor have their basic needs met, that the unemployed do not suffer from want, that the young are educated and the old are cared for. To do less is to fail in our love for neighbor. To do less is also to keep us from singing with joy: *I love you, Lord, my strength.*

"The commandments to love God with all one's heart and to love one's neighbor as oneself are the heart and soul of Christian morality.... These commands point out the path toward true human fulfillment and happiness. They are not arbitrary restrictions on human freedom. Only active love of God and neighbor makes the fullness of community happen. Christians look forward in hope to a true communion among all persons with each other and with God." U.S. Bishops, *Economic Justice for All* (1986) 64.

31st Sunday in Ordinary Time

Readings: Malachi 1:14—2:2, 8-10
1 Thessalonians 2:7-9, 13
Matthew 23:1-12

Faith gives us the promise of peace and makes known the demands of love. And what love demands is service: *The greatest among you will be the one who serves the rest.* The problem is that *selfishness blurs the vision of faith*, and so *we break faith with each other*, thereby *violating the covenant of our fathers.* We people of religion are all too often like the Pharisees, laying heavy loads on other people's shoulders without lifting a finger to budge them ourselves.

Instead of judging the poor, we should be serving them through our efforts on behalf of economic justice. Instead of criticizing those of other races, we should be serving them through our efforts on behalf of racial justice. Instead of ignoring the homeless, we should be serving them through our efforts on behalf of adequate housing for all.

May we live the faith we profess. Our faith tells us that we are all brothers and sisters: *Have we not all the one Father?* The way to live this faith is to build a human community of love and justice, and the first step in doing this is the acknowledgment of our failings and the offering of *a pure sacrifice for the forgiveness of our sins.*

"God's word proclaims the oneness of the human family—from the first words of Genesis, to the 'Come, Lord Jesus' of the Book of Revelation. God's word in Genesis announces that all men and women are created in God's image; not just some races and racial types, but all bear the imprint of the Creator and are enlivened by the breath of his one Spirit." U.S. Bishops, *Brothers and Sisters to Us* (1979) 25.

32nd Sunday in Ordinary Time

Readings: Wisdom 6:12-16
1 Thessalonians 4:13-18
Matthew 25:1-13

The theme of the Gospel is: *Be watchful and ready*. We are in a condition of awaiting something or someone important, and we don't know when the arrival will take place. Hence the advice: *keep your eyes open, for you know not the day or the hour*.

The liturgy combines this reading with a passage from Wisdom, suggesting that what we are awaiting is the arrival of wisdom: *he who watches for her at dawn shall not be disappointed*.

When will we finally understand what we need to know in order to live together as brothers and sisters? When will we get the wisdom to place the one true God ahead of our petty gods of power, possessions, and pleasure? When will we be inspired with the wisdom to overcome our social ills? We do not know when, and so we must *be watchful and ready*, otherwise the moment will pass us by.

One thing we do know: wisdom *makes her own rounds, seeking those worthy of her*. Those will not be found worthy who do not listen to the Scriptures, or to their own experiences, or to the sufferings of those around them. The message to them will be tragic: *I tell you, I do not know you*.

"We do not know the time for the consummation of the earth and of humanity, nor do we know how all things will be transformed. As deformed by sin, the shape of this world will pass away; but we are taught that God is preparing a new dwelling place and a new earth where justice will abide, and whose blessedness will answer and surpass all the longings for peace which spring up in the human heart." Vatican II, *Constitution on the Church in the Modern World* (1965) 39.

33rd Sunday in Ordinary Time

Readings: Proverbs 31:10-13, 19-20, 30-31
1 Thessalonians 5:1-6
Matthew 25:14-30

The Gospel parable is about a man entrusting his servants with his property, and the point it makes concerns the need for fidelity in caring for what belongs to the master.

God our master has left us with the earth, not to do with it what we want but to care for it even as we live off of its abundant riches. God created the land to support living things: What will happen when God returns to find so much land strip-mined, strip-cleared, eroded, and burdened with toxic waste? God created the waters to support living things: What will happen when God returns to find the oceans and rivers polluted with our garbage and chemical by-products? God created the air to support living things: What will happen when God returns to find smog and holes in the ozone? God created plants and animals to live on this wonderful earth and revel in its beauty: What will happen when God returns to find so many of them driven to extinction by our destructive practices?

Father of all that is good, keep us faithful in serving you. May we learn to care better for the Master's goods so that when the Master returns, we will hear those blessed words: *Well done! Come and share your master's joy.*

"Men and women bear a unique responsibility under God to safeguard the created world and by their creative labor even to enhance it. Safeguarding creation requires us to live responsibly within it, rather than manage creation as though we are outside it. The human family is charged with preserving the beauty, diversity and integrity of nature as well as fostering its productivity." U.S. Bishops, *Renewing the Earth* (1991) II,A.

34th Sunday in Ordinary Time: Christ the King

Readings: Ezekiel 34:11-12, 15-17
1 Corinthians 15:20-26, 28
Matthew 25:31-46

The very concept of Christ the King might seem rather triumphalistic in an age of expanding democratization of society. But look carefully at this king as portrayed in today's parable: he was hungry and thirsty and naked and ill and in prison. And who are his loyal subjects? They are those who give food to the hungry and drink to the thirsty, who welcome strangers and clothe the naked, who comfort the ill and visit prisoners. What a king and what a kingdom!

The goal of this king is not to oppress his subjects with his power but rather to *break the power of evil*: In this kingdom the evils of economic, medical, and criminal injustice are confronted and overcome by subjects who not only respect the *King of creation* but also *glory in his justice* and *live in his love*.

The kingdom that we celebrate today is *a kingdom of truth and life, a kingdom of holiness and grace, a kingdom of justice, love, and peace*. Those who respect truth and life, who live in holiness and grace, and who work to bring justice, love and peace, will *inherit the kingdom prepared for them from the creation of the world*.

"After we have obeyed the Lord, and in his Spirit nurtured on earth the values of human dignity, brotherhood and freedom, and indeed all the good fruits of our nature and enterprise, we will find them again, but freed of stain, burnished and transfigured, when Christ hands over to the father: 'a kingdom eternal and universal, a kingdom of truth and life, of holiness and grace, of justice, love, and peace.' On this earth that Kingdom is already present in mystery. When the Lord returns it will be brought into full flower." Vatican II, *Constitution on the Church in the Modern World* (1965) 39.

FEASTS

Immaculate Conception (December 8)

Readings: Genesis 3:9-15, 20
Ephesians 1:3-6, 11-12
Luke 1:26-38

Do not fear, Mary. You have found favor with God. This wonderful message of a sinless human being concerns, first, Mary herself. We rejoice in her holiness, and we acknowledge her special worthiness to be the mother of Christ. It concerns us as well, for *the image of the Virgin is found in the Church.*

Mary's sinlessness is a sign of the holiness that Christ has won for all of us. She was the first to enter that state of wholeness which awaits all those whom Christ will welcome into kingdom, all those whom *God chose ... to be holy and blameless.*

It should not go unnoticed that God opened the way for the coming of the Savior by preparing a sinless vessel. Perhaps we should learn from this as we seek to bring Christ to the world. The Immaculate Conception teaches us that we must clear the way to make room for Christ. We must rid the world of its evils, its denial of human dignity, its attacks on life, its disregard for the harmony of all creation. It is in ridding the world of injustice that we make room for the entrance of Christ.

"The Church in her apostolic work rightly looks to her who brought forth Christ, conceived by the Holy Spirit and born of the Virgin, so that through the Church Christ may be born and grow in the hearts of the faithful also. The Virgin Mary in her own life lived an example of that maternal love by which all should be fittingly animated who cooperate in the apostolic mission of the Church on behalf of the rebirth of men." Vatican II, *Constitution on the Church* (1964) 65.

Presentation of the Lord (February 2)

Readings: Malachi 3:1-4
Hebrews 2:14-18
Luke 2:22-40

They bring Jesus to the temple to be *presented to the Lord*, for he is *the Anointed of the Lord*. One way of responding to this event is to reflect on our own 'presentation of the Lord.' How do we present Jesus Christ to others? Is the Jesus we present to others a convenient cover for a life of personal misbehavior and social indifference, or is he *the king of glory* whose person and teachings should govern us individually and collectively? Do we present Jesus to others on such a pedestal that people can dismiss his example as unreasonable expectation, or is he *like his brothers in every way*, one of us, a brother human whose love of justice and peace can and should be imitated? Is the Jesus we present to others an indictment of them, or is he God's *saving deed displayed for all the peoples to see*, the Messiah who rescues us from our personal and social sinfulness? Is the Jesus we present to others a support for our dealings with death, our wars, abortions, and death penalties, or is he *a lamb without blemish (offered) for the life of the world*? Is the Jesus we present others a special 'god' for the privileged, or is he *the light of all peoples*, including people who are weak and outcast?

"God's Word, through whom all things were made, was himself made flesh and dwelt on man's earth. Thus he entered the world's history as a perfect man, taking that history up into himself and summarizing it. He himself revealed to us that 'God is love' (I John 4:8) and at the same time taught us that the new command of love was the basic law of human perfection and hence of the world's transformation. To those, therefore, who believe in divine love, he gives assurance that the way of love lies open to men and that the effort to establish a universal brotherhood is not a hopeless one." Vatican II, *Pastoral Constitution on the Church in the Modern World* (1965) 38.

St. Joseph (March 19)

Readings: 2 Samuel 7:4-5, 12-14, 16
Romans 4:13, 16-18, 22
Matthew 1:16, 18-21, 24

The Church celebrates the fact that God *entrusted our Savior to the care of St. Joseph. The Lord has put his faithful servant in charge of his household.* Joseph is special to us because he was faithful in his role as caretaker.

We, too, are caretakers. As individuals, we are responsible in different ways for the care of others. As members of the Church, we are responsible for the care of each other, of all people everywhere, and of the Good News of salvation. As human beings, we are responsible for the care of the earth.

We honor St. Joseph as *that just man, that wise and loyal servant, whom you placed at the head of your family.* He is an example to us, who should be just, wise, and loyal in our care for the world around us, the human world and the world of nature.

"Our faith teaches us that 'the earth is the Lord's' (Ps 24) and that wealth and private property are held in trust for others. We are trustees of God's creation, and as good stewards we are required to exercise that trust for the common good and benefit of our brothers and sisters."
U.S. Bishops, *The Right to a Decent Home* (1975) 10.

Annunciation (March 25)

Readings: Isaiah 7:10-14
Hebrews 10:4-10
Luke 1:26-38

Mary confronted an opportunity to be filled with the Spirit of God, and she said yes. She could choose to bring God's offer of salvation into the world, and she said yes. She could consent to the coming of the kingdom of God, and she said yes. Because of her yes, the world has never been the same.

What would the world be like if we were to say yes to Jesus Christ and to all he represents? Can you imagine a world in which people say yes to peace? in which they say yes to harmony among peoples? in which they say yes to equitable distribution of resources? in which they say yes to respect for the dignity of every individual?

Suppose we were, like Mary, to say yes to life! Such a simple yes, pronounced with Mary's total faith and carried out with Mary's dedication, would mean an end to the killing we carry out in so many different ways, as well as to the personal and institutional violence that leads to the killing.

Perhaps one day we will have said such a yes, and we will be able to repeat the words of the psalmist: *I announced your justice in the vast assembly.*

"The Father of mercies willed that the consent of the predestined mother should precede the Incarnation, so that just as a woman contributed to death, so also a woman should contribute to life. This contrast was verified in outstanding fashion by the Mother of Jesus. She gave to the world that very Life which renews all things, and she was enriched by God with gifts befitting such a role." Vatican II, *Constitution on the Church* (1964) 56.

Ascension

Readings: Acts 1:1-11
Ephesians 1:17-23
Mark 16:15-20

We usually think of faith as an attitude of trust and belief on our part: We trust God's word and believe its message. The Ascension is perhaps the expression of a different faith, God's faith in us. God-become-human could have remained on earth and done everything required for the coming of the kingdom. Instead, Jesus removed himself physically from the earth, making room for his followers. He trusted them, he believed in them, he had faith that, once they were filled with the Spirit, they would work effectively for the coming of the kingdom.

It remains for us to *go into the whole world and proclaim the good news to all creation.* It is our task to relieve suffering, to end war, to remove ignorance, to heal wounds, to eliminate divisions, to promote understanding, to spread love, to cause justice. We must tackle the problems of the world, and Jesus has stepped aside, so to speak, so as not to get in our way.

Why do you stand here looking up at the skies? Get busy! There is work to do!

"Christ's redemptive work, while of itself directed toward the salvation of men, involves also the renewal of the whole temporal order. Hence the mission of the Church is not only to bring men the message and grace of Christ, but also to penetrate and perfect the temporal sphere with the spirit of the gospel." Vatican II, *Decree on the Apostolate of the Laity* (1965) 5.

Birth of St. John the Baptist (June 24)

Readings: Jeremiah 1:4-10
1 Peter 1:8-12
Luke 1:5-17

We honor John the Baptist as a prophet sent *to prepare for the Lord a people well-disposed*, to *help God's people to walk the path of salvation.*

The prophets were people who, like Isaiah, had God's words placed in their mouths. *They investigated the times*, and through their reading of the signs of the times, they were able to declare God's justice.

John the Baptist had the task of preparing the people immediately before the arrival of the messiah. His message was one of repentance, change of life, metanoia. His baptism was a sign of change, of turning things around, in the direction of God.

The lesson of John the Baptist is that the world will receive Jesus Christ when it turns away from its violent and oppressive ways. It must allow the prophets *to turn the hearts of fathers to their children and the rebellious to the wisdom of the just.*

"In the face of the present-day situation of the world, marked as it is by the grave sin of injustice, we recognize both our responsibility and our inability to overcome it by our own strength. Such a situation urges us to listen with a humble and open heart to the word of God, as he shows us new paths towards action in the cause of justice in the world." Synod of Bishops, *Justice in the World* (1971) 29.

Sts. Peter and Paul (June 29)

Readings: Acts 3:1-10
Galatians 1:11-20
John 21:15-19

Peter and Paul were recognized already in the early church as the leaders of the community established by Jesus. Peter was the acknowledged first among the apostles; Paul led the translation of the movement into the world of the Gentiles.

Among the elements that distinguish Catholic Christianity from the rest of Christianity is the Petrine ministry, the acceptance of the unique role played by the successor to Peter, the bishop of Rome. Paul, the apostle to the peoples of the world, is also very special to that community that goes by the name of Catholic, universal. Together, these two apostles represent the internal organization and outward orientation of our Church.

Both men had pasts of which they had to repent: Peter denied Jesus as he went to trial, and Paul *went to extremes in persecuting the church of God and tried to destroy it.* They are witnesses to the power of God's grace, which transformed them into people who *love me more than these.* They provide us with hope that God's grace can transform the people of our day.

"Jesus Christ, the eternal Shepherd, established His holy Church by sending forth the apostles as He Himself had been sent by the Father. He willed that their successors, namely the bishops, should be shepherds in His Church even to the consummation of the world. In order that the episcopate itself might be one and undivided, He placed blessed Peter over the other apostles, and instituted in him a permanent and visible source and foundation of unity of faith and fellowship." Vatican II, *Constitution on the Church* (1964) 18.

Transfiguration (August 6)

Readings: Daniel 7:9-10, 13-14
2 Peter 1:16-19
Mark 9:2-10

The three disciples witnessed an amazing event. The carpenter's son from Nazareth who had become an itinerant teacher with a reputation for healing and doing other wonders was *transfigured before their eyes and his clothes became dazzlingly white.* It was a theophany to rival any of the appearances of Yahweh, before whom the people of Israel hid their faces lest they die.

The preface reminds us that the Church is the body of Christ, and that it will *one day share his glory.* What if this body of Christ, this Christian assembly, were to reveal its glory to the world! What if our clothes were to become dazzlingly white! What if we became such a holy and God-like community that our neighbors would be *overcome with awe!*

Jesus calls us to be a community of love, concerned more with the interests of others than with their own interests. He calls us to be a community of justice with a commitment to making the world a place of right living. He calls us to be a community of peace, at peace with each other and bringing peace to all around us. Were we truly that way, we would dazzle the world!

"The Church ... serves as a leaven and as a kind of soul for human society as it is to be renewed in Christ and transformed into God's family.... the Church not only communicates divine life to men, but in some way casts the reflected light of that life over the entire earth." Vatican II, *Constitution on the Church in the Modern World* (1965) 40.

Assumption (August 15)

Readings: 1 Chronicles 15:3-4, 15, 16; 16:1-2
1 Corinthians 15:54-57
Luke 11:27-28

The song that Luke puts in Mary's mouth when she visits Elizabeth speaks of a God who *has deposed the mighty from their thrones and raised the lowly to high places.* Mary herself is a prime example of the lowly raised to high places: a poor and simple girl, a virgin from an insignificant part of the world, raised to the status of Mother of God, and today raised *body and soul to the glory of heaven.*

There is an attractiveness about God raising the lowly that makes it pleasing for us to accept, at least theoretically. We react positively to the raising of a Mother Theresa from the status of lowly servant of the hopeless to that of Nobel Peace Prize winner. We are less attracted to the idea of God deposing the mighty from their thrones, especially if we live in the "First World" and in the country that boasts of being first in the world.

Mary said: *The hungry he has given every good thing, while the rich he has sent empty away.* This should come as good news to the poor, and should be of some concern to affluent Americans, who belong to the richest five percent of the world's population.

"Let the entire body of the faithful pour forth persevering prayer to the Mother of God and Mother of men. Let them implore that she who aided the beginnings of the Church by her prayers may now, exalted as she is in heaven above all the saints and angels, intercede with her Son in the fellowship of all the saints." Vatican II, *Constitution on the Church* (1964) 69.

Triumph of the Cross (September 14)

Readings: Numbers 21:4-9
Philippians 2:6-11
John 3:13-17

Isn't it amazing that we base our religion on an instrument of execution intended to bring the cruelest suffering and most humiliating death to the lowest of human beings, the dregs of society. We take images of that horrible instrument and we hang them as decorations in our houses, we make jewelry in its image, and we trace its image over our bodies whenever we pray.

We are a religion of the cross and of all that it stood for. We do not run away from suffering and death, but rather we transform them into salvation and resurrection. We do not run away from humiliation, but rather we joyfully accept humiliation for the sake of the glory of God. We do not run away from the lowest of human beings, but rather we embrace them as other Christs.

When I am lifted up from the earth, I will draw all men to myself, says the Lord. The powers of this world are nothing compared to the power of the cross of Christ.

"Christ in His boundless love freely underwent His passion and death because of the sins of all men, so that all might attain salvation. It is, therefore, the duty of the Church's preaching to proclaim the cross of Christ as the sign of God's all-embracing love and as the fountain from which every grace flows." Vatican II, *Declaration on the Relationship of the Church to Non-Christian Religions* (1965) 4.

All Saints (November 1)

Readings: Revelation 7:2-4, 9-14
1 John 3:1-3
Matthew 5:1-12

The saints are those who have *washed their robes and made them white in the blood of the Lamb*. They are those who lived not according to the civil religion of their day but according to the Good News of Jesus Christ. Their platform was the upside down world of the beatitudes:

The world sets up the rich in first place;
    Jesus put the poor on top of the world.
The world tells us to seek happiness at all cost;
    Jesus saw happiness in mourning.
The world values power over others;
    Jesus praised the meek.
The world encourages self-fulfillment;
    Jesus told us to work for justice.
The world says that the merciless succeed;
    Jesus proclaimed blessed the merciful.
The world announces: Go for the gold!
    Jesus taught us to keep our hearts pure.
The world honors the winners of wars;
    Jesus celebrated peacemakers.
The world sees the persecuted as losers;
    Jesus declared them the winners.

"Christians who take an active part in modern socioeconomic development and defend justice and charity should be convinced that they can make a great contribution to the prosperity of mankind and the peace of the world. Whether they do so as individuals or in association, let their example be a shining one. After acquiring whatever skills and experience are absolutely necessary, they should in faithfulness to Christ and His gospel observe the right order of values in their earthly activities. Thus their whole lives, both individual and social, will be permeated with the spirit of the beatitudes, notably with the spirit of poverty." Vatican II, *Constitution on the Church in the Modern World* (1965) 72.

All Souls (November 2)

Readings: Job 19:1, 23-27
1 Corinthians 15:51-57
John 6:37-40

We have a wonderful tradition in Christianity of praying for the souls of all the dead. Notice that we pray for all the dead: *strengthen our hope that all our departed brothers and sisters will share in his resurrection.* We don't separate the rich from the poor, or the black from the white, or the male from the female; we don't leave out those who were criminals or had AIDS or were illiterate; we don't give special prayer privilege to the powerful or the intellectual or the ecclesiastical. This is **All** Souls Day. We pray for them **all**. We wish them **all** eternal life.

What will it take for us to create a world in which we treat the living with as much respect and equality as we treat the dead? Why can't we find a way to be as tolerant of souls living in bodies as we are of disembodied souls?

"God, who has fatherly concern for everyone, has willed that all men should constitute one family and treat one another in a spirit of brotherhood. For having been created in the image of God, who 'from one man has created the whole human race and made them live all over the face of the earth' (Acts 17:26), all men are called to one and the same goal, namely, God Himself." Vatican II, *Constitution on the Church in the Modern World* (1965) 24.

Dedication of St. John Lateran (November 9)

Readings: 2 Chronicles 5:6-10, 13—6:2
1 Corinthians 3:9-13, 16-17
Luke 19:1-10

Although the basilica of St. John Lateran is the cathedral of the Holy Father in Rome, today's liturgy focuses not on the Petrine ministry but on the place of God's abode, the temple. The first reading is about Solomon's temple, and the Gospel tells of Jesus coming to stay in the home of Zacchaeus.

Writing to the Corinthians, Paul asks them: *Are you not aware that you are the temple of God, and that the spirit of God dwells in you?* Notice his use of the singular: *the temple of God is holy, and you are that temple.* He has in mind the community of God's people as the temple of God: *from living stones, your chosen people, you built an eternal temple to your glory.*

Is this temple (the People of God) only for the presence of God? What else is there in this temple? Are there false gods as well, such as the gods of wealth and power? Do the people in this temple worship the one true God, or do they bow down before other gods, such as economic and political systems? Do the people in this temple work hard at *creating its beauty from the holiness of our lives?*

"The Church has more often been called the edifice of God.... This edifice is adorned by various names: the house of God in which dwells His family; the household of God in the Spirit; the dwelling place of God among men; and, especially, the holy temple. This temple, symbolized by places of worship built out of stone, is praised by the holy Fathers and, not without reason, is compared in the liturgy to the Holy City, the New Jerusalem. As living stones we here on earth are being built up along with this City." Vatican II, *Constitution on the Church* (1964) 6.